Poems United

A Commonwealth Anthology

Edited by Diana Hendry and Hamish Whyte

Scottish Poetry Library . Black & White Publishing

First published in 2007 by

Scottish Poetry Library
5 Crichton's Close, Edinburgh EH8 8DT
www.spl.org.uk

and

Black & White Publishing
99 Giles Street, Edinburgh EH6 6BZ
www.blackandwhitepublishing.com

ISBN 978-1-84502-140-5

Designed by Iain McIntosh
Printed and bound in Poland www.polskabook.pl

Glasgow
CITY COUNCIL

Scottish
Arts Council

Find out more about
Scotland's bid for the
Commonwealth Games
and register your support at
www.glasgow2014.com

GLASGOW2014
COMMONWEALTH GAMES
CANDIDATE CITY

Commonwealth Countries

Africa

Botswana, Cameroon, The Gambia, Ghana, Kenya, Lesotho, Malawi, Mauritius, Mozambique, Namibia, Nigeria, Seychelles, Sierra Leone, South Africa, Swaziland, Tanzania, Uganda, Zambia **Americas** Belize, Bermuda, Canada, Falkland Islands, Guyana, St Helena **Asia** Bangladesh, Brunei Darussalam, India, Malaysia, Maldives, Pakistan, Singapore, Sri Lanka **Caribbean** Anguilla, Antigua & Barbuda, Bahamas, Barbados, Dominica, Grenada, Jamaica, Montserrat, St Kitts & Nevis, St Lucia, St Vincent, Trinidad & Tobago, Turks & Caicos Islands **Europe** Cyprus, England, Gibraltar, Guernsey, Isle of Man, Jersey, Malta, Northern Ireland, Scotland, Wales **Oceania** Australia, Cook Islands, Fiji, Kiribati, Nauru, New Zealand, Niue, Papua New Guinea, Samoa, Solomon Islands, Tonga, Tuvalu, Vanuatu

contents

index of poets

Poetry is under one's nose, waiting to be discovered

Charles Causley

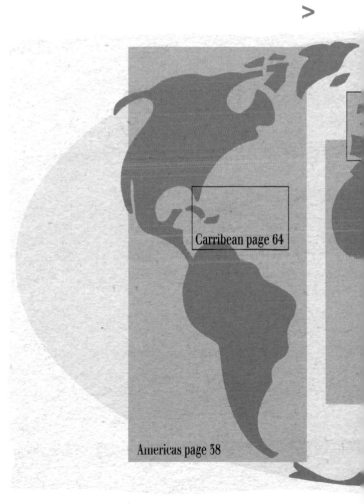

Carribean page 64

Americas page 38

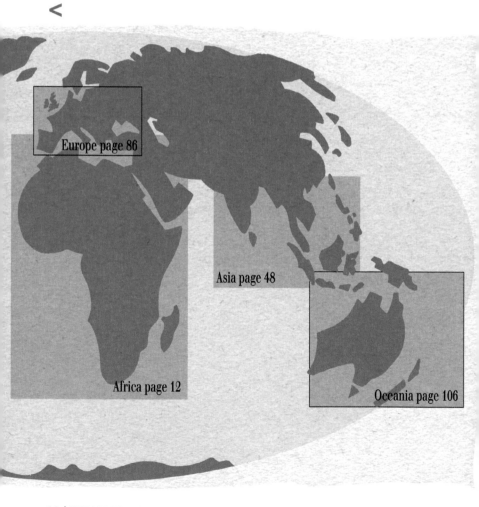

Europe page 86

Asia page 48

Africa page 12

Oceania page 106

SELECTING POEMS for this anthology — trying to find a poem from each country of the Commonwealth — was a geography lesson (not to mention a history lesson) in itself. We often had the atlas out, scouting for tiny islands whose names we knew but not exactly where they were. Turning page after page made us realize what a vast, worldwide organization the Commonwealth is. And reading poems from all these countries took us on a journey — not just armchair travelling but a safari of the imagination. What is it like to live on a Caribbean island or in Mozambique or Bangladesh? We wondered about the many different peoples, landscapes, climates, songs, languages — and, perhaps most importantly, we wondered how it would be to live in these countries as a child. We were very pleased to be able to include some poems by young people themselves, from the Falkland Islands, Papua New Guinea and Sri Lanka.

It wasn't easy finding the poems — some countries seem to be more poetical than others — but we managed — with some help (thank you, Pat Bryden, Stewart Conn, Liffy Grant, Suchen Christine Lim, Grace Nichols, Neil Philip, Enda Ryan of the Mitchell Library and especially Robyn Marsack of the Scottish Poetry Library who had the original idea for the book, and her staff) — to track down poets and poems from almost every country. We failed with only three: British Virgin Islands, Cayman Islands and Norfolk Island, though we feel there must be poems out there. And we don't know what we would have done without John Gallas's wonderful anthology of world poetry, *The Song Atlas*.

The Fact Finder, which you'll find at the end of each section of the book, and which was compiled by Liffy Grant, will tell you all sorts of fascinating facts and figures about the Commonwealth countries. What we've tried to do is choose poems that at the very least have a flavour or tang of the country they come from. You'll find poems about families and friendships, animals and birds, flowers, jungles, rivers, oceans, islands — a host of things, not to mention the weather and a tractor.

We would like to think that wherever in the world this book is read, the countries can speak to each other — a poem from Nigeria, for example, speaking to a poem from New Zealand or Gibraltar.

We chose the title for this collection, 'Poems United', partly because the words had the ring of a football team, but mainly because we feel that poetry and language have the power to bring people together everywhere.

Diana Hendry
Hamish Whyte
October 2006

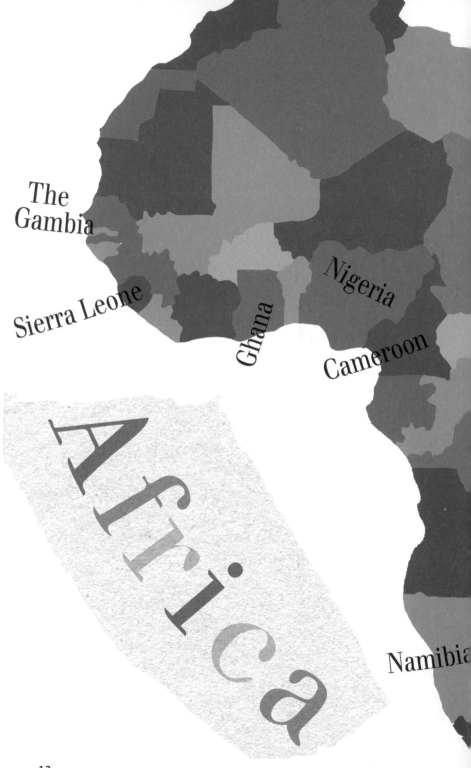

The
Gambia

Sierra Leone

Ghana

Nigeria

Cameroon

Africa

Namibia

Uganda

Kenya

Tanzania

Seychelles

Zambia

Malawi

Mozambique

Botswana

Mauritius

South Africa

Swaziland

Lesotho

All the Same

Me mahogany
colour of strength
mopped and
topped
by kinky curls
of Kgalagadi
ancestry
but hairy
all the same
nostrils wide
Receptive
like antelope
of the savannas
nose broad
trait
of species
negroid
but nosey
all the same
heart
shape of the continent
of people
denied
people
cheated
people
mistreated
people
robbed
people
rising
having risen
able to
feel
love
need
all the same ...

you frigid pink
blancmange
crowned by sisal
freely flowing
to the nape
coppertoned
in the glint
of the golden orb
regal
in the domain
of sky blue
eyes
emerald
treasures
of lands
forgotten
lips
ruby of empires
of antiquity
heart
shape of new
generations
wanting
to understand
to want –
wanting
all the same
all other things
being equal
do you
want
to be
my friend?

Barolong Seboni

The Free Bird

The bird who passes over there
The light bird
Who flaps his wings
And slices through the air over there in the horizon,
Doesn't own a thing in the world,
But how freedom
Makes him pretty!

And he lives singing
On the branch
This beautiful travelling bird
Who gives rhythm to the seasons

For nothing is worth more than freedom:
It is the most dignified of all fortunes
The freedom which the bird
Who lives on the branch enjoys!

Freedom and its sacred fire
Natural freedom
O sacred freedom
Which should be enjoyed
By any being
In his simple state!

Claude-Joseph M'bafou-Zetebeg

Sleep-song

Sleep and sleep well, little one:
but open your eyes
and look at me for a minute
before you go to sleep.

I want to see the thing
the thing that shines inside
inside your clear new eyes
and shines at me.

Now shut your eyes, little one:
I think I saw
what I wanted to see.
Sleep now, and sleep well.

Anonymous

Senior Lady Sells Garden Eggs

I love the lit corners of your kerosene smile,
your sympathy soft as new-boiled nkontommire*
no whines come between you and this world, and
your large elbows take all the knocks possible. O
senior lady sits in the rain, sells
garden eggs with a sense of grace
under a wide hat wider than all my markets,
and the chewing-stick brushes
memories long dry with their own strength.
She meets life's one-wheel screams
with the subtlest roars in the land:
if you can't stop the rain
you can throw your own water up, or
store the biggest tank underground. Can
I too not give my floods direction, as
I watch you watch the deaths go by,
    watch the children grow like sugar-cane,
hard and sweet with your own dying.
I love the quiet corn boiling
as you look through its steam to far worlds,
your mind in a maze it loves, in prayers
spread on the waters like boats broad and dry.
Senior Lady sells garden eggs,
fights in her own way only when she must, and
she must; a slight almost hidden glint, in her eye,
        a tightening of the shoulders,
        a face set like shield or armour.
The water is flowing, stand back, you
can't be hard to a hard world forever, and
the great face shines
like the sun through morning mist, and strangely
the rain is caught in her large hands and sent home.

Kojo Laing

*named after the coco yam plant
and often used in Ghanaian cooking

Wife of the Husband

His snores
protect the sleeping hut
but the day's
load
and the morrow's
burden
weigh heavily over
the stooping mother as she

    sweeps the hut
    bolts the pen
    tidies the hearth
    buries the red charcoals
    and finally seeks
    her restless bed

His snores
welcome her to bed
four hours to sunrise
His snores rouse her from bed
six sharp
Arise
O, wife of the husband!

Micere Githae Mugo

Peace, Rain, Plenty

Mountains plumb.
Bush whispering.
Men unnettled.
= Peace.

Dust gurgling.
Green bubbling.
Men dazzled.
= Rain.

Roads rolling.
Men coming.
Men going.
= Plenty.

Anonymous

Sunrise above Naisi

The sun streaks above Lake Chilwa
like a glittering orb in a Hollywood film;
the sea-sick breeze that caresses the land
breathes peace into my mind
and my heart coos and ululates
at the clear skies spanning Chiradzulu
across St Mary's and Blantyre beyond;
thin clouds glide across the sky
like butterflies in a prize collection.

I say, 'Amen' to the land of the living
and to the surging tide of the works of man's hands,
to the jokes of the woodcutter heaving his merchandise
and to the wave of limousines taking children to school
sliding below concealed drives
like centipedes around an ant-hill.

'Amen' to the 'sig' tune of summer
this persistent murmur of a brook on Zomba mountain
the incessant chirrup of a bird
perched on a swaying pine;
the distant rumour of a wind
sails like a muted jet
above the shadow of this man-made forest.

We are honoured
by all that is good in this land
and mine is not a voice crying in the wilderness
but a soul aching for infinity.

Felix Mnthali

it was / so hot ...

it was

so hot

that

the flowers

had

to use

their

colours

as fans.

Malcolm de Chazal

AFRICA

If you want to know me

If you want to know me
examine with careful eyes
this bit of black wood
which some unknown Makonde* brother
cut and carved
with his inspired hands
in the distant lands of the North.

This is what I am
empty sockets despairing of possessing life
a mouth torn open in an anguished wound
huge hands outspread
and raised in imprecation and in threat
a body tattooed with wounds seen and unseen
from the harsh whipstrokes of slavery
tortured and magnificent
proud and mysterious
Africa from head to foot
this is what I am.

Noemia de Sousa

* *The Makonde, who live in Northern Mozambique
and Southern Tanzania, are famed for their expressionist
wood sculpture.*

Animal Freedom

Giraffe: Days change
When life is hard
   Forests become bad
   When leaves fall
My neck is long
   No place to hide

Elephant: I lived in a forest
In the thick bush
Beyond the bushy grass
   Before the bulldozer
Then the caterpillar
   Uprooted the trees
Taken by unkind man
   Chasing us away
   With evil firing lorry.

Giraffe: Sleeping never seen
Walking continues
No time for rest
   Thunder often raining
With red hail
Firing light
   Morning and evening
Socking hearts
Smelling niff
As snuff or curry.

Elephant: Manggeti, bornforest
   Elephant-parents long lived
   Peacefully!
   Sharing waters
   In black man's pool
   During the hot drought.

Nondakofa Tujeni

Confession

Like a mischievous boy,
I peep through the door-hole,
beholding a naked old man, half asleep,
spent,
on the bamboo bed;

and I raise a fire alarm,
false,
for the man to scuttle away
to his shrine, his *ikenga*[1], his life-wire, his soul,
into the cold claws of the harmattan[2];

while I,
showing broken teeth of laughter,
sneak into his hut
to emerge later with large rounded yams,
hurriedly treading on scattered corns,
mouth bursting with red-ripe nuts
and eyes squinting
sentinel-wise
like a mischievous boy.

Edward C. Okwu

[1] *a wood carving which symbolises
personal achievement or success*
[2] *a dry and dusty wind*

Out

Bolt the door

Disconnect the doorbell

Cut the phone and modem line

Nail the letterbox shut

Blackout the windows

Detach the antennae

Nitin Shroff

AFRICA

Careful!

pull

a

rope

and

the

rope

pulls

in

the

forest

and

with

the

forest

leopards

come

to

town.

Anonymous

The child who was shot dead by soldiers at Nyanga

The child is not dead
the child lifts his fists against his mother
who shouts Afrika! shouts the breath
of freedom and the veld
in the locations of the cordoned heart

The child lifts his fists against his father
in the march of the generations
who shout Afrika! shout the breath
of righteousness and blood
in the streets of his embattled pride

The child is not dead
not at Langa nor at Nyanga
not at Orlando nor at Sharpeville
nor at the police station at Phillippi
where he lies with a bullet through his brain

The child is the dark shadow of the soldiers
on guard with rifles, saracens and batons
the child is present at all assemblies and law-givings
the child peers through the windows of houses and
                                    into the hearts of mothers

this child who just wanted to play in the sun at
                                    Nyanga is everywhere
the child grown to a man treks through all Africa
the child grown into a giant journeys through the
                                    whole world

Without a pass*

Ingrid Jonker

*Under the system of apartheid, all black South Africans had to
carry pass books. It was similar to a passport but also contained
information about permission granted or refused for that person to
be in a certain region outside his/her 'homeland'.

You

Back from being
with you –
the bush rustles –
empty –
the sky stands –
empty –
the wind moves –
empty

Back from being
with you –
my heart –
empty –
my words –
empty –
my house –
empty

Back from being
with you –
I remember –
something –
I think up –
something –
I see –
something

My grassthatch –
your hair –
my windows –
your eyes –
my door –
your mouth –
my land –
your otherwise

Back from being
with you –
the bush –
your words –
the sky –
your beauty –
the wind –
your thoughts

Back from being
with you –
my heart –
yours –
my words –
yours –
my house –
you

Back from being
with you –
I remember –
words –
I think up –
thoughts –
I see –
beauty

Anonymous

The Ten-Day Visitor

Yay! A Visitor! Day one.
Dish him up rice and coconut
in a coconut hull.
Welcome, Mr Visitor!

Yay! A Visitor! Day two.
Butter him up with milk and ghee.
If Mr Visitor behaves himself,
oblige Mr Visitor!

Whoh! A Visitor! Day three.
Nothing left. Well,
just three pinchy helpings
warmed up for Mr Visitor!

Whoh! A Visitor! Day four.
Hand him a hoe.
This is an hoblique hint –
Go Home, Mr Visitor!

Hm. A Visitor. Day five.
He's skinny as a needle.
Everyone's whispering and pretending not to.
Mr Visitor is making snorting noises.

Hm. A Visitor. Day six.
Everyone's hogging scraps and pretending not to.
Everyone's lurking in nooks,
hiding from Mr Visitor!

Gawd. A Visitor. Day seven.
Mr Visitor is a bloody pain.
If the roof catches fire,
blame Mr Visitor!

Gawd. A Visitor. Day eight.
Please come and say goodbye!
If you see him take one bloody step outside
yell at him 'Bye!' 'Seeya!' 'Go home, Mr Visitor!'

Booo! A Visitor! Day nine.
Please go away forever, Mr Visitor.
Please don't ever pass this way again!
Please, Mr Visitor, don't ever come back!

Booo! A Visitor! Day ten.
Guess who: kick kick, slap slap,
punch punch. Get him out of here!
Haha! It's Mr Visitor!

Anonymous

Night Illusion

Coming by last night
we were charmed by
silvery moonlight over
vast green tea fields.
The road was a ribbon
of white in the darker shade
of the tea fields.

Round the bend lay a
small hillock, rounded
and soft like a man's buttock.
It slept there so quietly.
We must come and see it
again tomorrow.

The next morning, the purring of the
car's engine was harsh.
It disturbed the stillness around.
The road now was sandy and hard
in the glare of the sun
and seemed to disturb
the great green tea fields.

Round the bend lay our hillock.
But look! Who has wrenched
my heart and made me
stand still?
A great grey gash has been
torn in the side of the hill
as if a lion had sunk its
gory teeth in the soft human
flesh and torn a large chunk out.
Bald and uglily grinning
it stands, helpless, like an
old grey man with a toothless face.
This is the sand pit for
the tea factory over there.

> The emerald of the grass shines
> and stretches
> but cannot hide the
> man-made nakedness of its
> side.

Tejani

My dugout flibbles . . .

My dugout flibbles
flat out down the river.
Monkeys yawl and chitter
tree by tree by tree.
Ah, what's happened,
Jungle-Boss?

> *The wee monkey's bust his leg*
> *and everybody's bawling.*

Ah, River-Boss,
zip that paddle
and go tell mum
her wee monkey's crying:
the wee monkey's bust his leg
and everybody's bawling.

Anonymous

Africa
Fact Finder

✳ Capital
✳ Population
✳ Languages

Botswana
✳ Gaborone
✳ 1,785,000
✳ Setswana, Shona, English

Botswana is a landlocked state in southern Africa.
Did you know?
Approximately 80 per cent of its land mass is made up of the Kalahari desert where the Kalahari bushmen have lived for thousands of years.
The Tsodilo Hills in the Kalahari desert have over 4,500 paintings dating back over thousands of years.

Cameroon
✳ Yaounde (constitutional): Douala (economic)
✳ 17,000,000
✳ English, French
Cameroon in central Africa borders Nigeria, Chad, the Central African Republic, the Republic of the Congo, Gabon, Equitorial Guinea and the Gulf of Guinea.

Did you know?
The Portuguese gave Cameroon its name 'Camaroës' when they landed in 1472 and found huge numbers of giant shrimp there.
There are over 24 major African languages spoken in Cameroon as well as French and English.

The Gambia
✳ Banjul
✳ 1,600,000
✳ English, Mandinka, Fulani, Wolof
Gambia lies on the west coast of Africa and is entirely surrounded on the land by Senegal.
Did you know?
It is one of the smallest countries in Africa and was declared independent in 1965 when, with no official explanation, *The* was added to its name.
Alex Haley, author of the prize-winning book *Roots*, based the story on one of his ancestors from the Gambian village of Juffure, who was forced into slavery in the eighteenth century.

Ghana
✳ Accra
✳ 22,000,000
✳ English, Hausa, Akan
Ghana borders the Ivory Coast to the west, Burkino Faso in the north, Togo to the east and the Gulf of Guinea to the south.
Did you know?
In 1964, the Akosombo dam was built on the Volta River creating Lake Volta, which is one of the world's largest artificial lakes.
Evidence of habitation in Ghana can be dated back between 30,000 and 40,000 years.

Kenya
✳ Nairobi
✳ 34,000,000
✳ Swahili, English
Kenya is in eastern Africa bordering the Indian Ocean and the countries of Tanzania, Uganda, Sudan, Ethiopia and Somalia.
Did you know?
The Masai Mara National Game Reserve stretches over 1510 square kilometres and one of its most spectacular sights is the annual wildebeest migration during July and August, when thousands of these ungainly beasts move north from the Serengeti Plain.
The Great Rift Valley which runs the length of Kenya was formed 20 million years ago.

Lesotho
✳ Maseru
✳ 2,000,000
✳ Sesotho, English, Zulu
Lesotho is landlocked entirely by South Africa.
Did you know?
Lesotho is also known as the 'Mountain Kingdom', the 'Kingdom in the Sky' and the 'Roof of Africa'.
A dinosaur is named after Lesotho; the Lesothosaurus was one metre long and lived around 200 million years ago. You can see dinosaur footprints in many sites in the country.

Malawi
✴Lilongwe
✴12,000,000
✴English, Chichewa, Lomwe
Malawi is in central Africa and bordered by Tanzania, Zambia and Mozambique.
Did you know?
Blantyre, Malawi's largest city, was named after the birthplace of the Scottish missionary and explorer, David Livingstone. Scotland continues to have a special relationship with Malawi which began with the work of David Livingstone when he went to Africa as a missionary doctor. Scots have been working with the people of Malawi for almost 150 years to help develop health and education systems.

Mauritius
✴Port Louis
✴1,220,000
✴English, French, Creole, Hindi
Mauritius is an island nation in the southwest Indian Ocean, east of Madagascar.
Did you know?
When Mark Twain visited Mauritius in 1896 he was so impressed by its beauty that he said, 'God first made Mauritius and from it, he created Paradise.'

Mauritius was the dodo bird's only habitat – this flightless bird became extinct in 1681.

Mozambique
✴Maputo
✴19,500,000
✴Portuguese, Makua, Tsonga, English
Mozambique is in southeastern Africa and bordered on the east by the Mozambique Channel in the Indian Ocean.
Did you know?
The Zambezi river flows into the Indian Ocean via Mozambique having completed its 2,700 mile course starting in north-western Zambia. Mozambique was originally colonised by the Portuguese at the end of the fifteenth century, became independent in 1975 and joined the UK Commonwealth in 1995.

Namibia
✴Windhoek
✴2,000,000
✴English, Afrikaans, German, Ovambo
Namibia is on the coast of southwestern Africa.
Did you know?
The sand dunes of the Namib desert, which is said to be the world's oldest desert, are among the highest in the world.

The Hoba Meteorite near Grootfontein is the world's largest meteorite – it is estimated that it fell on earth around 80,000 years ago.

Nigeria
✴Abuja
✴131,000,000
✴English, Creole, Hausa, Yoruba, Ibo, Fulani
Nigeria borders Benin in the west, Chad and Cameroon in the east, Niger in the north and the Gulf of Guinea in the south.
Did you know?
Biafra, which had declared itself independent from Nigeria in 1966 was finally re-integrated three years later but the civil war left a legacy of over one million dead .

Seychelles
✴Victoria
✴81,000
✴Creole, English & French
The Seychelles is an archipelago lying east of Kenya.
Did you know?
It is made up of 115 granite and coral islands – the Aldabra Atoll which is part of the Outer Island group, has the world's largest population of giant tortoises.

Sierra Leone
✴Freetown
✴5,000,000
✴English, Krio-English, Mende, Temne
Sierra Leone lies on the Atlantic coast of West Africa between Guinea and Liberia.
Did you know?
Krio-English is the first language for only 10 per cent of the population but understood by over 95 per cent.
Those British who were against the slave trade established the province of Freetown, Sierra Leone's capital, in 1787 to provide a safe haven for those who had escaped slavery.

South Africa *(joined the Commonwealth in 1931, left in 1961, rejoined 1994)*
✴Pretoria (administrative); Cape Town (legislative)
✴45,000,000
✴Afrikaans, English, Swazi, Xhosa, Zulu
South Africa is located at the southern tip of the African continent and borders Botswana, Namibia, Zimbabwe, Mozambique and Swaziland.
Did you know?
In 1998, a human skeleton which was over three and a half million years old was

discovered at the Sterkfontein Caves in Mpumalanga. Desmond Tutu the South African bishop and Nobel Peace Prize winner who is best known for his work against apartheid was quoted as saying, 'When the missionaries came to Africa they had the Bible and we had the land. They said, "Let us pray." We closed our eyes. When we opened them we had the Bible and they had the land.'

Swaziland
✳Mbabane
✳1,100,000
✳siSwati/English
Swaziland is a small, landlocked country in southern Africa embedded between South Africa in the west and Mozambique in the east.
Did you know?
It is the smallest country in the continent. Every year, the people of Swaziland celebrate

Ncwala, the Festival of the First Fruits which begins with a journey to the Indian Ocean to collect ocean foam. When the water gatherers return to the king's residence the ceremonies begin and continue for six days.

Tanzania
✳Dar es Salaam
✳37,000,000
✳Kiswahili/English, Nyamwez
Tanzania lies on the coast of east Africa with Mount Kilimanjaro and the Serengeti National Park its most famous national landmarks.
Did you know?
Archaeological remains almost 2 million years old were found at the Olduvai Gorge on the Serengeti Plain which have given scientists many clues about how the earliest humans lived.
Ujiji in Tanzania was where Henry Stanley finally met David Livingstone in 1871

and reputedly greeted him with the words, 'Doctor Livingstone, I presume'.

Uganda
✳Kampala
✳28,000,000
✳English, Swahili, Luganda
Uganda is a landlocked country bordered by Sudan, Kenya, Tanzania, Rwanda and the Republic of the Congo.
Did you know?
Its highest point is Margherita Peak on Mount Stanley standing at 5,110 metres.
Lake Victoria in Uganda is one of the chief sources of the river Nile which is 4184 miles long; the river and its tributaries flow through a total of nine countries.

Zambia
✳Lusaka
✳10,800,000
✳English, Bemba,

Nyanja, Tonga
Zambia is a landlocked country in southern Africa bordered by eight nations.
Did you know?
It was named after the Zambezi River which flows through the country. Before 1964, the country was called Northern Rhodesia, after Cecil Rhodes, the Englishman who built his massive fortune from diamond-mining. The skull of 'Rhodesian Man' was found in Kabwe, Zambia in 1921 – the skull is thought to be between 125,000 and 300,000 years old.

Africa
Fact Finder

Bermuda

Belize

Guyana

Falkland Islands

Canada

St Helena→•

Americas

When a fish ...

When a fish
screws
slimy up
out of
the long
dark
river-
downness
and
bubbling
says
down
there
blub
in the
long
dark
deepness
blub
there's
an
alli-
gator
blub
oh
believe
that
fish.

Anonymous

Emily Hurricane

Woke up this morning
to a breakfast sky,
fed the kitten marmalade,
had some sunshine in my tea
and then went out to greet the day,
met Miss Emily Hurricane.

She said
Wouldn't you like to swim in the sky,
sail with the trees as they go whizzing by,
dance with the rooftops as they go bubbling?
Wouldn't you like to swim in the sky?

She had silver hair
but it was kind of wild,
electricity for eyes
and a crackling laugh,
ranting and raving
like she was crazy.

She kept singing to me
Wouldn't you like to swim in the sky,
sail with the trees as they go whizzing by,
dance with the rooftops as they go bubbling?
Wouldn't you like to swim in the sky?

I asked her,
'Why are you howling
outside my windows?'
She answered,
'Rounding up beaches to herd away
and deliver to a better place.'

And the beaches like white sheep but sad,
their beauty blemished with tar and debris,
were elated to run away with her
and find a safer home at the bottom of the sea.

As they left she whistled,
Wouldn't you like to swim in the sky,
sail with the trees as they go whizzing by,
dance with the rooftops as they go bubbling?
Wouldn't you like to swim in the sky?

I shouted in reply,
'Maybe someday I'd like to join the beaches
at the bottom of the sea.'
As she disappeared I heard her sing,
'If you ever make it to the bottom of the sea
you can join us as we dance, the beaches and me.'

Alan Smith

Snake Woman

I was once the snake woman,

the only person, it seems, in the whole place
who wasn't terrified of them.

I used to hunt with two sticks
among milkweed and under porches and logs
for this vein of cool green metal
which would run through my fingers like mercury
or turn to a raw bracelet
gripping my wrist:

I could follow them by their odour,
a sick smell, acid and glandular,
part skunk, part inside
of a torn stomach,
the smell of their fear.

Once caught, I'd carry them,
limp and terrorized, into the dining room,
something even men were afraid of.
What fun I had!
Put that thing in my bed and I'll kill you.

Now, I don't know.
Now I'd consider the snake.

Margaret Atwood

Balancing Act

He sees the beauty below
As he flies overhead,
Those who look up
See his beauty light the sky.
The functional feathers
In his long delicate wings
Use the wind beneath him.
In elegance he is a king.
So free is he in the sky
To roam from place to place,
His aesthetically perfect body floats
Between his artistic wings of lace.
On and on he goes,
Swooping and diving,
Weaving and dipping,
For speed he's striving.
Over the water,
Around the trees
With no need at all to fly over cities.
He's a country bird
And there he'll stay
If we just leave him
To his play.

Donna Triggs

Wha Me Mudder Do

Mek me tell you wha me mudder do
wha me mudder do
wha me mudder do

Me mudder pound plantain mek fufu
Me mudder catch crab mek calaloo stew

Mek me tell you wha me mudder do
wha me mudder do
wha me mudder do

Me mudder beat hammer
Me mudder turn screw
she paint chair red
then she paint it blue

Mek me tell you wha me mudder do
wha me mudder do
wha me mudder do

Me mudder chase bad-cow
with one 'Shoo'
she paddle down river
in she own canoe
Ain't have nothing
dat me mudder can't do
Ain't have nothing
dat me mudder can't do

Mek me tell you

Grace Nichols

Americas

from **The Name of the Island**

in memoriam
Marguerite Delphine Ritch Blandford
(B. 1898? ST HELENA – D. 1976 SYDNEY)

My grandmother's island is

wrapped in its own ocean and a fog

　　that whispers and sings to itself

since lighthouses and watermarked maps

　　put reefs out of business and

exiles no longer smoulder into their diaries

　　in the gloom of rock and rain.

Yvette Christianse

✳Capital
✳Population
✳Languages

Belize
✳Belmopan
✳280,000
✳English, Creole, Spanish, Mayan
Belize is located in central America and borders Mexico and Guatemala.
Did you know?
The first inhabitants were Maya and Carib Indians and it was part of the great Mayan empire which can be traced back over 4,000 years.
The 'Blue Hole' in the centre of the Lighthouse Reef Atoll* is a circular hole 1,000 feet in diameter, over 400 feet deep and is visible from outer space.
(*Atolls are coral reefs which surround a lagoon in open sea.)

Americas
Fact Finder

Bermuda
✳Hamilton
✳65,000
✳English
Bermuda lies east of the USA.
Did you know?
Its 181 islets lie along the southern edge of a submerged volcanic mountain.
Bermuda is named after Juan de Bermudez, a Spanish seafarer who discovered the island in 1503.

Canada
✳Ottawa
✳33,000,000
✳English/French
Canada forms the northern portion of North America and is the second largest country in the world.
Did you know?
Lake Superior is the world's largest freshwater lake – more than seven per cent of Canada's area is made up of fresh water

whilst it also has the longest coastline of any country in the world. The lowest recorded temperature is claimed by Snag in the Yukon Territory where a temperature of minus 63 degrees Celsius was reached during the winter of 1947.

Falkland Islands
✳Stanley
✳2,900
✳English
The Falklands lie just off the tip of South America.
Did you know?
Although it consists of two main islands – East and West – the Falklands are made up of another 700 smaller islands.
The Falkland Islands are an overseas territory of the United Kingdom but they are also claimed by Argentina, which invaded the islands in 1982; UK armed forces regained

control in June of the same year.

Guyana
✳Georgetown
✳765,000
✳English, Creole and Hindi
Guyana lies in the north-east of South America and is approximately the same size as Great Britain.
Did you know?
Guyana is the third smallest, and the only English-speaking, country in South America. It takes its name from a native word meaning 'land of many waters'.
Gold was discovered in 1879 in Guyana – the Omai gold mine is one of the largest open pit gold mines in South America.

St Helena
✳Jamestown
✳7,000
✳English
St Helena lies midway between South America and Africa in the South Atlantic Ocean.
Did you know?
St Helena was uninhabited when it was discovered by the Portuguese in 1502. Napoleon Bonaparte was exiled to the island after his defeat at the Battle of Waterloo – he lived there from 1815 until his death in 1821.

Asia

Pakistan

India

Bangladesh

Maldives

Sri Lanka

Brunei Darussalam

Malaysia

Singapore

Mon-doria

Mon-doria,
    my heart's river,
        overflowing
            with joy and song,
      you skip softly,
    sweetly, through light
and shadow in
    the Sunderban.*
        Your salaams touch
            towns and hamlets
      on your endless
    travels. You call
us, ceaselessly
    murmuring. Moss
      and a thousand
        weeds turn the swift
      whirlpool of dreams,
    desires and hopes.
Your waters flow
    in faith, blowing
      like a sari
        in the wind, strong
      and calm to reach
    your noble end:

to make deserts
    bloom – paradise
        here on earth now.
          Mon-doria,
      my heart's river,
    overflowing
with joy and song.

*Sunderban: the name means 'beautiful forest',
a forested region of Bangladesh.*

Rashida Islam

A twist of hair ...

A twist of hair
stitches softly
puffed flour
on a pan.

I lower my
pinced fingers
at it in a thin
flour-cloud.

Carefully. The hair
must not prick
deeper or
slip away.

And the flour
must not hush
off the edge
by breath or dab.

A delicate matter
needs the same
exact line
to put right.

Anonymous

A Pair of Glasses

It's with glasses
in front of my eyes and on my nose
that I see the world.

I need glasses
to see my neighbour and the washerman
and the postman,
to see that Radha and Krishna walking along the road,
or to see Radha as Radha
and Krishna as Krishna.

Glasses are the door
through which I talk to a stranger,
a guest, a friend.
Through their glass I speak
to children, flowers,
and God.

Glasses for my day-dreams,
and for my cradle-songs.

For my unspoken word
and my unsung song.
Glasses.
Glasses for me.

In my childhood
I had no glasses.
All great men wear glasses.

All wearers of glasses are great.
My childhood—without glasses.
The textbook Gandhiji,
the cane-wielding math teacher,
and Appunni, the postman.
Or, for that matter,
behind every pair of glasses that's taken off
a great man.
In my childhood
I had no glasses.

But today,
like the gods and prophets
who have haloes,
the scholar who has a bald head,
or the rich man who has a potbelly,
I too have
a pair of glasses.

Savithri Rajeevan

Translated from Malayalam by
K. Ayyappa Paniker and Arlene Zide

Home

Home is the place where the diseased world dies at the door,
where the floor and carpet are worn by familiar feet,
where you can close your eyes and nobody says you are blind.

Home is where you don't have to be polite and sing cane-sweet
　　　song to coat bitterness,
where familiarity accepts you in its security,
where you know that love still breathes somewhere,
where your wife and children keep the other half of you.

When the rain broadcasts the glass face of the fields and moves
　　　the tidemark of the canals,
when you do not know where to go,
home is where they never say 'no'.

The small cottage that sits cosily under the palms,
the atap*, brown with time and age hangs to the field,
the complaining hinges and wet stairs,
home is you
and where you hope to die.

Mohamad Haji Salleh

*palm leaf thatched roof

The Muiveyo Cow

Long ago, when the Sultan sat
on his Sultanic seat
and ruled
with a kind of
fatherly fright,
herds of cows
happily wandered
and munched
the island of Male.

The Sultan's Sultanic
Herd wandered and munched
with a kind of
special wandering, munching
Pride
of Place
and the people
treated them
with a kind of
winking respect.

Now, one day
the Second Secretary
of the Sultan's Sultanic
Secret Service
found a cow
from the Royal Herd
swimming
in a mooing kind of way
round and round a blue lagoon
at Muiveyo
on the other side
of the island.   >

<

Swimming and mooing,
in fact,
in a kind of
frightening way.

He hurried back to tell the Sultan,
who was sitting
on his Sultanic seat
and ruling.
'Heavens!' said the Sultan.
'Call the Royal Sultanic
Council Cabinet Consultative
Commission!'
And they did.

And the Royal Sultanic
Council Cabinet Consultative
Commission
discussed,
in a lengthy way,
how to save the cow
who was swimming and mooing
in the blue lagoon
on the other side
of the island.

However,
although they
discussed the matter
in a lengthy way
for a long time
they came to no
agreement,
conclusion
or decision.

The Sultan said,
'Send the
        Second Secretary
of my Sultanic
        Secret Service
back
to the blue lagoon
at Muiveyo
on the other side
of the island
to find out
in a more
        informative way
about
the mooing
        and swimming
of my Royal Cow.'
And they did.

The Second Secretary
of the Sultanic
    Secret Service
was gone
for a long time.
When he returned,
the Sultan said,
'What did you find
at the blue lagoon
at Muiveyo
on the other side
of the island?'

And the Second Secretary
of the Sultanic
    Secret Service said:
'The cow
has finished his swim.'

The Royal Sultanic
Council Cabinet
Consultative Commission
sighed
in a smiling kind of way
and dispersed
to play draughts.

And the Sultan's
    Sultanic Herd
happily wandered
and munched
once more
the island of Male,
and the Sultan sat
on his Sultanic Seat
and went on
ruling.

Anonymous

I am Glad to be Up and About

I am glad to be up and about
              this sunny morning,
Walking the raised path between fields,
While all around me
Are cheerful folks harvesting potatoes.

I am glad to be away from books,
Broadcasts, and the familiar smells,
And the unending pursuit of a livelihood.

Small boys on their way to school
Trail their toes through the stripped soil,
And pounce with joy
Upon the marble-size potatoes
              left behind by the harvesters,
And with these fill their satchels.

Asia

One voice is raised in song,
While the men, hunkering on their heels,
Move up in a line like pirates
To uncover the heaps of buried treasure,
And transfer them to baskets.

And girls who should be playing with dolls
Unload the baskets into sacks
Which tonight or tomorrow night
Will be speeding in a groaning truck
To Karachi, a thousand miles away.

And this week or the following week,
Bilious businessmen and irate wives
And their washed and prattling children,
Will sit down at uncounted tables
And hastily devour the potatoes I see
With never a thought for these
Fields, these men, and this sunny morning.

Taufiq Rafat

First anniversary

May 1998
for Granny on the first
anniversary of her passing

Your sight strong
Your body frail
I said to you
Go towards the Bright Light –
just keep going.

You planned your leave
to the last detail –
Joss paper,
Red strings,
Pearls on silver
If to light the way.

Better before noon,
Food for generations.
Sovereigns for the girls,
Titles for the boys.
Tradition and habits
Hide innermost thoughts.

One should have daughters,
you said to your daughter,
And she to hers,
And she, only cried.
Meticulous was your plan,
Amitabha was goodbye.

Madeleine Lee

Killer Waves

The killer waves made their way,
In to our island on that day,
It was sunny and bright,
The twenty-sixth day of December.
Why did the sea be so wicked to us?
That we children loved so much,
Is it because we take its fish?
From the sea which gives it life.

The beach was a place the children loved,
Why was the sea so cruel to us?
And brought tears to our eyes so much,
Who can give me an answer to that?

Today is a day we all are crying,
Trying to help the ones who are alive,
I am begging you sea don't do this again,
Because we love you please never again.

Yachitha Sahitra Samaraweera

✳Capital
✳Population
✳Languages

Bangladesh
✳Dhaka
✳150,000,000
✳Bangla, Bihari, Hindi and English
Bangladesh lies adjacent to the Bay of Bengal and has one of the world's densest populations.
Did you know?
Cyclones occur frequently in Bangladesh – the 1970 cyclone is thought to have killed up to five hundred thousand people.
Bangladesh has the largest coastal mangrove forest in the world in Sundarbans National Park.

Brunei Darussalam
✳Bandar Seri Bagawan
✳379,000
✳Malay, English and Chinese
Brunei is located on the island of Borneo in south-east Asia and surrounded by East Malaysia apart from the coastline with the South China Sea.
Did you know?
From the fourteenth to the sixteenth centuries Brunei Darussalam was the seat of a powerful sultanate

Asia
Fact Finder

extending over Sabah, Sarawak and the lower Philippines. The current sultan of Brunei represents one of the oldest continuously ruling dynasties in the world. Brunei Darussalam means 'Abode of Peace'.

India
* New Delhi
* 1,065,500,000
* Hindi, English

The south-east Asian nation of India has a coastline of over 7,000 kilometres.

Did you know?
It has the highest population of the Commonwealth countries, second only to China in the world. It has the biggest Hindu temple in the world, The Srirangam Temple in Tiruchirappalli, Tamil Nadu.

Malaysia
* Kuala Lumpur
* 24,425,000
* Malay, English, Chinese, Tamil

Malaysia is made up of two regions divided by the South China Sea. West Malaysia shares a border to the north with Thailand while East Malaysia borders Indonesia and Brunei.

Did you know?
Malaysia has the world's only revolving monarchy with nine state sultans, each taking a turn at being the ruler for five years at a time.
The Malaysian jungle is believed to be 130 million years old with the world's oldest rainforests. The forests of Sabah are the home of trees towering over 100 metres high.

Maldives
* Malé
* 339,000
* Dhivehi, English

The Maldives form an island nation situated south-west of Sri Lanka in the Indian Ocean.

Did you know?
The islands are thought by many archaeologists — including Thor Heyerdahl, the Norwegian scientist and explorer — to have been settled first by an ancient race of sun-worshipping people called the Redin.
The Maldives consist of 1,190 coral islands, grouped into 26 major atolls.

Pakistan
* Islamabad
* 165,000,000
* Urdu, Punjabi, Sindhi, Pushtu, English

Pakistan is located in south-east Asia and borders Iran, Afghanistan, China, India and the Arabian Sea.

Did you know?
Its highest mountain is K2 in the Karakoram range. K2 is the second highest mountain in the world standing at 8,617 metres.

Singapore
* Singapore
* 4,500,000
* English, Chinese (Mandarin), Malay, Tamil

Singapore is an island city-state and the smallest south-east Asian country, situated on the southern tip of the Malay peninsula.

Did you know?
According to Malayan legend, a Sumatran prince encountered a lion – considered a good omen – on Temasek and went on to found Singapura or Lion City; it is still known as 'Lion City' today even though lions have never inhabited the island.

Sri Lanka
* Colombo
* 19,000,000
* Sinhala, Tamil, English

Sri Lanka is a tropical island lying south of India.

Did you know?
Sri Lanka was formerly known as Ceylon, changing its name in 1948 when it achieved independence. It has several nicknames including 'Teardrop of India', 'Resplendent Isle' and 'Pearl of the Orient'.

Caribbean

Turks & Caicos
Islands

Anguilla

Antigua
& Barbuda

St Kitts & Nevis

Montserrat

Dominica

St Lucia

St Vincent & the Grenadines

Grenada

Barbados

Trinidad & Tobago

Rum Jumbee

John Boy walkin in de night all alone
Stop and look cause he hear a soft moan.

Saw a baby jumbee sittin near a tree
He say, 'John Boy come and keep me company.

Long, long ago, there was thousans of us
Now eletric lights come an we are dispussed.

We had excellent times in de buryin grung
Because in dat place no human hang arung.

We used to trick ya parents upon de tird day
After their loved one had passed away.

We would laugh and roar in our ghostly woice
After we see big people running away from us.

We would take funny shapes and make spooky sounds
As soon as the evening sun went dung.

Caribbean

We did rule Anguilla from duss till dawn
Then hide in de tamarin trees at morn.

Now me oldfolks dead. Oh cuss de eletric light
Not a jumbee friend nowhere in sight.

Ah beg ya tell ya leaders, whatebber demm do
Dat we is part of de enwirement too.

Who could be so cruwell to stop de fun
Of de boys and girls after set of de sun?

Please tell dem turn off de current real fass
Cause I – Rum Jumbee – is one of de lass.'

John Boy walkin in de night all alone
No longer afaraid of dat jumbee soft moan.

Patricia J. Adams

Children, Children

Children, children.
Yes, Mama?
Where did you went to?
To see Granpa.
What did he give you?
Bread and patata.
Where did you put it?
Upon de ledge.
Suppose it drop.
I don't give a rap.

Anonymous

Caribbean

Morning Break

Girls in white blouses, blue skirts,
boys in blue trousers, white shirts,
singing, swinging, screeching, reaching,
hooking wasps, riddle-saying,
ring-playing –
Bayhanna, bayhanna, bayhanna, bay –
If your teacher scolds you
listen to what you say
That's the way to bayhanna, bayhanna, bay.

Lamppost schoolmaster in grey jacket,
grey tale of wild Abaco hog and donkey;
mild worry, calm hurry,
stiff bones and cane;
ring-playing –
round the green apple tree
where the grass grows so sweet,
Miss Della Miss Della,
your true lover was here,
and he wrote you a letter
to turn 'round your head.

First bell, all frozen.
Second bell, instant motion,
Disappear.

Telcine Turner

doodle durdle

doodle durdle caw caw
doodle durdle doo

doodle durdle coo coo
doodle durdle doo

doodle durdle caw caw
doodle durdle blam

doodle durdle coo coo
doodle durdle bang

if a crow flies with pigeons
he gets shot too.

Anonymous

Caribbean

In the Woods

Blat … blat … water
levers leaves …
trees shift
with an easy fever …
insects tick …

Scritch … scritch … cabbagetrees
fret each other …
the fig umbrellas itself …
an owl hoos
down the green dark …

Spitter … spitter … swallows
slip through
the steel
white sky's
pieces.

Anonymous

Caribbean

The candy-throated Carib flaps …

The candy-throated Carib
flaps along the treetops

brushing heaven and
the ceiling of the world

its eyes eating
the crammed air

like years like certainty
like years of certainty

like colour like kings
like breath flaps

along the treetops brushing
heaven and the world

The candy-throated Carib
lies on the cut field

weighed in mud and
the stubble of the earth

the ants eating
his full eyes

like years like nothing
like years of nothing

like colour like kings
like breath lies

on the cut field weighed
in mud and earth.

Anonymous

A Story about Afiya*

Afiya has fine black skin
that shows off her white clothes
and big brown eyes that laugh
and long limbs that play.
She has a white summer frock
she wears and washes every night
that every day picks on something
to collect, strangely.

Afiya passes sunflowers and finds
the yellow fringed black faces there,
imprinted on her frock, all over.
Another time she passes red roses
and there the clustered bunches
are, imprinted on her frock.   >

*Afiya: a Swahili name, meaning health, is
pronounced Ah-fee-yah*

<

She walks through high grass and sees
butterflies and all kinds
of slender stalks and petals
patterned on her back and front
and are still there, after
she has washed her dress.

Afiya stands. She watches
the sharp pictures in colour,
untouched by her wash.
Yet, next morning, every day,
the dress is cleared and ready,
hanging white as new paper.

Then pigeons fly up before her
and decorate her dress
with their flight and group design.
Afiya goes to the zoo;
she comes back with two tigers
together, on her back and on her front.

She goes to the seaside;
she comes home with fishes
under ruffled waves
in the whole stretch of sea
imprinted on her dress.

She walks between round and towered
boulders and takes them away,
pictured on her.

Always Afiya is amazed,
just like when she comes home
and finds herself covered
with windswept leaves
of October, falling.

James Berry

The Boy of the House

The ruin of the house, he lies on his stomach,
    womanless.
The boy is in water, frog-like, his mouth tastes of
    seaweed.
He is looking at the rose garden, it's not there
No longer at the front of the house –
Of what used to be the house …

The rose garden is now at the bottom of the sea
And the boy throws a line, then another
To prevent more of the house drifting away.
He does this instead of growing into middle age,
    or going abroad:
The boy is a great source of worry.

E.A. Markham

makeme

the
the
the
he
he
his
monkey
arsehole
higher
more
climbs
goes
shows

Anonymous

A Sea-Chantey

Là, tout n'est qu'ordre et beauté,
Luxe, calme, et volupté.

Anguilla, Adina,
Antigua, Cannelles,
Andreuille, all the l's,
Voyelles, of the liquid Antilles,
The names tremble like needles
Of anchored frigates,
Yachts tranquil as lilies,
In ports of calm coral,
The lithe, ebony hulls
Of strait-stitching schooners,
The needles of their masts
That thread archipelagoes
Refracted embroidery
In feverish waters
Of the sea-farer's islands,
Their shorn, leaning palms,
Shaft of Odysseus,
Cyclopic volcanoes,
Creak their own histories,
In the peace of green anchorage;
Flight, and Phyllis,
Returned from the Grenadines,
Names, entered this sabbath,
In the port-clerk's register;
Their baptismal names,
The sea's liquid letters,

Repos donnez à cils …
And their blazing cargoes
Of charcoal and oranges;
Quiet, the fury of their ropes.
Daybreak is breaking
On the green chrome water,
The white herons of yachts
Are at sabbath communion,
The histories of schooners
Are murmured in coral,
Their cargoes of sponges
On sandspits of islets
Barques white as white salt
Of acrid Saint Maarten,
Hulls crusted with barnacles,
Holds foul with great turtles,
Whose ship-boys have seen
The blue heave of Leviathan,
A sea-faring, Christian,
And intrepid people.

Now an apprentice washes his cheeks
With salt water and sunlight.

In the middle of the harbour
A fish breaks the Sabbath
With a silvery leap.
The scales fall from him
In a tinkle of church-bells;

>

<

The town streets are orange
With the week-ripened sunlight,
Balanced on the bowsprit
A young sailor is playing
His grandfather's chantey
On a trembling mouth-organ.
The music curls, dwindling
Like smoke from blue galleys,
To dissolve near the mountains.
The music uncurls with
The soft vowels of inlets,
The christening of vessels,
The titles of portages,
The colours of sea-grapes,
The tartness of sea-almonds,
The alphabet of church-bells,
The peace of white horses,
The pastures of ports,
The litany of islands,
The rosary of archipelagoes,
Anguilla, Antigua,
Virgin of Guadeloupe,
And stone-white Grenada
Of sunlight and pigeons,
The amen of calm waters,
The amen of calm waters,
The amen of calm waters.

Derek Walcott

Flight of the Firstborn

He streaks past his sixteenth year
small island life stretched tight
across his shoulders
his strides rehearsing city blocks
college brochures
airline schedules
stream excitedly through his
newly competent hands
his goodbyes like blurred neon
on a morning suddenly gone wet

I'm left stranded
on a tiny patch of time
still reaching
to wipe the cereal from his smile

Peggy Carr

Carnival Rhapsody

Beat dem drums
 Boys, beat dem drums,
  Fast and loud and sweet,
   Dey go ge we consolation,
   Dey go ease we sufferation,
  Down Frederick Street,
Down Frederick Street,

So beat dem drums
Boys, beat dem drums,
'Til Federation come
 Den we go jump in time
  To the Creole rhyme,
   Around de town.
        Around de town.

     And beat dem drums
      Boys, beat dem drums,
       'Til de Jour-Vert Monday comes
      When de Judge jump up,
      In de parson's frock,
    And de Doctor play de clown.

  So beat dem drums
   Boys, beat dem drums,
  Look! Ah feel de rhythm in me spine,
 Ah feel de rhythm,
 In me chac-chac wine,
Shaking me far behind.

 And beat dem drums
  Boys, beat dem drums,
    Ah feel de rhythm in me soul,
      Ah feel de rhythm in me Creole blood,
       E go stap wid me 'til ah ole.
        E go stap wid me 'til ah ole.

Knolly La Fortune

Caribbean

Listen to the Beat of the Sea

Come walk with me along the sea
Along the road that no cars travel
Just the birds and me
And listen to the beat of the sea.

The never ending cadence of the sea
A rhythm beyond you and me
No words are needed, no special time
Chords created by a greater mind.

Booming sounds like a roar
Then soothing crescendos as
The waves hit the shore
The repertoire is endless.

Come walk with me along this sea
On the empty road or on the beach
Hear only the music and tranquility
And listen to the beat of the sea.

Dale Marie Witt

* Capital
* Population
* Languages

Anguilla
* The Valley
* 12,000
* English

Anguilla lies at the northern end of the Leeward Islands in the Caribbean Sea and consists of five islands.

Did you know?
The first known colonisers were Amerindians, descendants of the indigenous people of Guyana, who settled on these islands about 3,500 years ago. The Amerindians called the island 'Malliouhana', the sea serpent, because of its long, thin shape (Anguilla is the Spanish and Italian word for eel).

Antigua & Barbuda
* St John's
* 73,000
* English, Creole

Antigua and Barbuda is one of the largest and most populous of the Leeward Islands in the Caribbean Sea.

Did you know?
It claims to have a 'beach for every day

of the year' and, not surprisingly, relies heavily on tourism for its economy.
Highest point on the island is 402 metres – and called Boggy Peak!

Bahamas
* Nassau
* 314,000
* English, Creole, French Creole

The Bahamas is an archipelago of about 700 islands in the northern Caribbean.

Did you know?
From the late 1600s to the early 1700s, the 'Golden Age of Piracy', the Bahamas was 'home' to many pirates including the infamous Blackbeard. The motto of the Bahamas is 'Pirates expelled, Commerce restored'. The writer Ernest Hemingway caught a tuna in the Birnini waters weighing a colossal 233 kg!

Barbados
* Bridgetown
* 270,000
* English, Creole (Bajan)

Barbados is the most easterly of the Caribbean islands, situated south of St Lucia and north of Trinidad and Tobago.

Did you know?
It was so-named by

the Portuguese sailors who landed there in 1563 and discovered the huge Banyan tree with roots hanging like beards - 'los barbados' meaning the 'bearded ones'.

Dominica
* Roseau
* 75,000
* English, French Creole

Dominica is an island nation in the Caribbean Sea situated south of Guadeloupe and north of Martinique.

Did you know?
One of the world's largest thermal lakes is to be found in the Morne Trois Pitons National Park, aptly named Boiling Lake.

Grenada
* St George's
* 80,000
* English, French Creole

Grenada is the most southerly of the Windward Islands in the Eastern Caribbean.

Did you know?
Grenada, also known as the spice islands, as it is an important supplier of nutmeg, mace and other spices.
Much of Grenada was devastated by Hurricane Ivan in 2004 when winds of over 260 kilometres per

hour (160 mph) hit the island.

Jamaica
* Kingston
* 2,650,000
* English, Creole

Jamaica is the third-largest Caribbean island and lies south of Cuba and west of Haiti.

Did you know?
Jamaica has nearly 3,000 varieties of flowering plants, including 800 species found nowhere else in the world. Two hundred species of wild orchid are indigenous to the island.
Ackee, the Jamaican national fruit, is often eaten for breakfast but beware… if it is opened before it is ripe it gives off a poison which can be fatal.

Montserrat
* Plymouth
* est. 4,500 (since volcanic eruption of 1995)
* English

Montserrat is one of the Leeward Islands in the Eastern Caribbean and lies south-west of Antigua and north-west of Guadeloupe.

Did you know?
The first recorded name for Montserrat was 'Alliouagana', derived from a prickly bush found on the island by the Carib people. Much of the island was

Caribbean
Fact Finder

devastated when the Soufriere Hills Volcano erupted in 1995 – it was the first eruption in 350 years.

St Kitts & Nevis

* Basseterre
* 42,000
* English, Creole

St Kitts and Nevis lies in the northern part of the Leeward Islands in the Eastern Caribbean.

Did you know?
The island was named Saint Christopher after the saint (but the British shortened it to St Kitts). The name Nevis comes from the Spanish for snow (*nieves*) as clouds on the mountains were said to look like snow, 'Our Lady of the Snows'.

St Lucia

* Castries
* 165,000
* English, French Creole

St Lucia is part of the Windward Islands group which form an arc jutting out from the Eastern Caribbean into the Atlantic, and lies north of Barbados.

Did you know?
Although small, St Lucia has produced two Nobel prizewinners: the late Sir W. Arthur Lewis who was awarded a Nobel prize for Economics in 1979 and the poet Sir Derek Walcott who was awarded a Nobel Prize for Literature in 1992.

St Vincent

* Kingstown
* 120,000
* English, Creole

St Vincent and the Grenadines is one of the countries of the Eastern Caribbean lying close to the end of the Caribbean chain and north of Grenada.

Did you know?
The Caribs who lived in St Vincent before it was colonised by the British called the island Yurumein which meant 'the beauty of the rainbows in the valleys'.

Trinidad & Tobago

* Port of Spain
* 1,300,000
* English, Creole, Hindi

Trinidad & Tobago are the most southerly Caribbean islands and lie off the coast of Venezuela; together they measure 2,000 square miles.

Did you know?
In 1997, a mud volcano (there are lots on the island) erupted in the village of Piparo on Trinidad with mud flying up to 150 feet in the air!

Most Tobagonians are of African descent while Trinidad is the most cosmopolitan society in the Caribbean; its population made up of people from Asia, Africa and Europe.

Turks & Caicos Islands

* Grand Turk (Cockburn Town)
* 20,000
* English

The Turks and Caicos Islands form the southern tip of the Bahamas chain in the north of the Caribbean chain.

Did you know?
To this day, there is no agreement as to which explorer landed in these islands first, Christopher Columbus in 1492, or Ponce de León.

John Glenn, the first American astronaut to orbit the earth in February 1962, 'splashed down' in the Atlantic near the islands – Glenn's debriefing took place on Grand Turk and he is quoted as saying 'I don't know what you could say about a day in which you have seen four beautiful sunsets'.

Isle of Man

Northern Ireland

Scotland

England

Wales

Guernsey→

Jersey→

←Gibraltar

Europe

Malta

Cyprus

Golden-Green Leaf[1]

    land of lemon and olive
    land of hug and joy
    land of pine and cypress,
    of young men and love
    golden-green leaf
    thrown into the ocean

    land of dried meadow
    land of embittered Madonna
    land of *livas*[2], Hades, loss,
    of fierce weather and volcanoes
    golden-green leaf
    thrown into the ocean

    land of laughing girls
    land of drunken boys
    land of dream and welcome
    Cyprus of love and dream
    golden-green leaf
    thrown into the ocean

Leonidas Malenis

[1] *from the Greek*
[2] *land of hot wind*

Earthed

Not precisely, like a pylon or
A pop-up toaster, but in a general
Way, stuck in the mud.

Not budding out of it like gipsies,
Laundry lashed to a signpost, dieting on
Nettles and hedgehogs,

Not lodged in its layers like badgers,
Tuned to the runes of its home-made walls, wearing
Its shape like a skin,

Not even securely rooted, like
Tribesmen tied to the same allotment, sure of
The local buses,

But earthed for all that, in the chalky
Kent mud, thin sharp ridges between wheel-tracks, in
Surrey's wild gravel,

In serious Cotswold uplands, where
Limestone confines the verges like yellow teeth,
And trees look sideways.

Everything from the clouds downwards holds
Me in its web, like the local newspapers,
Routinely special,

Or Somerset belfries, so highly
Parochial that Gloucestershire has none, or
Literate thrushes,

Conscientiously practising the
Phrases Browning liked, the attitude Hughes noticed,
Or supermarkets

Where the cashiers' rudeness is native
To the district, though the bread's not, or gardens,
Loved more than children,

Bright with resourcefulness and smelling
Of rain. This narrow island charged with echoes
And whispers snares me.

U. A. Fanthorpe

The Rock

That space on the form – Place of Birth –
reminds me of the looming rock
where I was born: Gibraltar.
Where Dad in cravat and cavalry twill,
his dark blue Chevvy as wide as the street,
pursued the dental nurse who scoured his teeth
three times – his keenness masked
by Scottish dour.

Family lore says Mum, huge with me,
fainted into a barrow of fruit.
'Very good, very good,' cackled the vendors
hauling her from crushed oranges –
'it's a boy, very strong.'
But Dad said I was left on the doorstep –
a wailing souvenir of Gib
from the Barbary apes.

Europe

The prize was soon carried to Dad's old home –

Ayr, with Arran looming over us.

Still by the sea, I grew up a Scot,

bred but not northern-born.

Less British than the vendors

with their olives and lemons, Union Jacks

that snap and fade in bleached noon light

above the rock I don't remember.

Neil McCrindle

Cosmic Text

get high
    bring the wind
        cloud

get
high & bring
    the cloud
  with the rain

get
   high
&
   pull
the cloud down

& the rain
& the rain
& the rain

the rain
the rain
the rain
the rain
the rain
the rain
the rain

```
rain        rain            rain            rain
rain        rain            rain            rain
rain        rain            rain            rain
rain        rain            rain            rain
rain        rain            rain            rain
r           ai               n
ra          i                               n
r           a                i              n
r           a                              in
ra           in             r             ain
r           ain            ra              in
r           ai                              n
ra           in            r             ain
r           ai               n           rain
rain        r               ai              n
r
                            ai              n
            r
  a
                            i
                                            n
  i
            r                               n
r                           a
  ain
                                           ra
                            i
            n
```

Dom Sylvester Houédard

The Harvest of the Sea

Hear us, O Lord, from Heav'n Thy dwelling place.
Like them of old, in vain we toil all night.
Unless with us Thou go, Who art the Light;
Come then, O Lord, that we may see Thy face.

Thou, Lord, dost rule the raging of the sea.
When loud the storm and furious is the gale;
Strong is Thine arm, our little barques are frail;
Send us Thy help; remember Galilee.

Our wives and children we commend to Thee
For them we plough the land and plough the deep,
For them by day the golden corn we reap,
By night, the silver harvest of the sea.

Sow in our hearts the seeds of Thy dear Love,
That we may reap Contentment, Joy and Peace;
And, when at last our earthly labours cease
Grant us to join Thy Harvest Home above.

W. H. Gill

Do you know who Whatsisname is?*

Have you seen him? It's like a madman
That he passes us in his car.
One of these days, he'll have an accident…
That… Whatsisname!

You know him well – a couple of years ago,
We saw him in the market on a bench.
With his car, he frightens me to death…
That Whatsisname.

His brother, they say, is a dope,
And his sister resembles him like two drops of water.
She passed yesterday and said 'Hello!' to you
With Whatsisname.

They all live at La Collinette –
You know – at the end of the little road!
Are you talking about Alexander Barette?
You've got him – that's him alright – that Whatsisname!

Joan Tapley

* from Jèrsiaise

Children Playing

Children dance on the sands,
on the thin skin of evening, hands
scattering bats and shadows, feet
pressing the delayed, sweet
hours like harvested grapes
into the sheltered redness of
the centre of the earth.

Children drumming their mirth
in the face of a large sun falling
hopelessly into the sea.

Riding the moon like a white horse over
the static housetops and the charcoal trees.

The night is open on the world and breathes.

John Cremona

Europe

Personal Helicon*

for Michael Longley

As a child, they could not keep me from wells
And old pumps with buckets and windlasses.
I loved the dark drop, the trapped sky, the smells
Of waterweed, fungus and dank moss.

One, in a brickyard, with a rotted board top.
I savoured the rich crash when a bucket
Plummeted down at the end of a rope.
So deep you saw no reflection in it.

A shallow one under a dry stone ditch
Fructified like any aquarium.
When you dragged out long roots from the soft mulch
A white face hovered over the bottom.

Others had echoes, gave back your own call
With a clean new music in it. And one
Was scaresome for there, out of ferns and tall
Foxgloves, a rat slapped across my reflection.

Now, to pry into roots, to finger slime,
To stare, big-eyed Narcissus, into some spring
Is beneath all adult dignity. I rhyme
To see myself, to set the darkness echoing.

Seamus Heaney

* *name of a mountain made famous by Greek
mythology which became an emblem of inspiration to poets*

Canedolia: An Off-Concrete Scotch Fantasia

oa! hoy! awe! ba! mey!

who saw?
rhu saw rum. garve saw smoo. nigg saw tain. lairg saw lagg.
rigg saw eigg. largs saw haggs. tongue saw luss. mull saw yell.
stoer saw strone. drem saw muck. gask saw noss. unst saw cults.
echt saw banff. weem saw wick. trool saw twatt.

how far?
from largo to lunga from joppa to skibo from ratho to shona from
ulva to minto from tinto to tolsta from soutra to marsco from
braco to barra from alva to stobo from fogo to fada from gigha to
gogo from kelso to stroma from hirta to spango.

what's it like there?
och it's freuchie, it's faifley, it's wamphray, it's frandy, it's sliddery.

what do you do?
we foindle and fungle, we bonkle and meigle and maxpoffle. we
scotstarvit, armit, wormit, and even whifflet. we play at crosstobs,
leuchars, gorbals, and finfan. we scavaig, and there's aye a bit of
tilquhilly. if it's wet, treshnish and mishnish.

what is the best of the country?
blinkbonny! airgold! thundergay!

and the worst?
scrishven, shiskine, scrabster, and snizort.

Europe

listen! what's that?
catacol and wauchope, never heed them.

tell us about last night
well, we had a wee ferintosh and we lay on the quiraing. it was
pure strontian!

but who was there?
petermoidart and craigenkenneth and cambusputtock and
ecclemuchty and corriehulish and balladolly and altnacanny and
clauchanvrechan and stronachlochan and auchenlachar and
tighnacrankie and tilliebruaich and killieharra and inverannach
and achnatudlem and machrishellach and inchtamurchan and
auchterfechan and kinlochculter and ardnawhallie and
invershuggle.

and what was the toast?
schiehallion! schiehallion! schiehallion!

Edwin Morgan

Cynddylan on a Tractor

Ah, you should see Cynddylan on a tractor.

Gone the old look that yoked him to the soil;

He's a new man now, part of the machine,

His nerves of metal and his blood oil.

The clutch curses, but the gears obey

His least bidding, and lo, he's away

Out of the farmyard, scattering hens.

Riding to work now as a great man should,

He is the knight at arms breaking the fields'

Mirror of silence, emptying the wood

Of foxes and squirrels and bright jays.

The sun comes over the tall trees

Kindling all the hedges, but not for him

Who runs his engine on a different fuel.

And all the birds are singing, bills wide in vain,

As Cynddylan passes proudly up the lane.

R. S. Thomas

Europe
Fact Finder

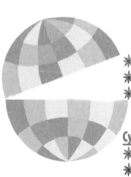

✳Capital
✳Population
✳Languages

Cyprus
✳Nicosia
✳800,000
✳Greek, Turkish, English

Cyprus is an island nation in the eastern Mediterranean sea, south of Turkey.

Did you know?
Cyprus is said to be the birthplace of Venus (Aphrodite), the Greek goddess of love.

Nicosia, the capital of Cyprus, is the only divided capital in the world, split between the internationally-recognized Cypriot government to the south and the Turkish-Cypriot community to the north.

England
✳London
✳52,000,000
✳English

England occupies most of the southern two-thirds of Great Britain and is bordered by Scotland to the north and Wales to the west.

Did you know?
U. A. Fanthorpe (who wrote 'Earthed') was awarded a CBE in 2001 for her services to poetry as well as the Queen's Gold Medal for Poetry in 2003.
The Poet Laureate who is appointed by the king or queen and writes poems for special occasions continues to be partly paid in wine! The tradition was started by King James in 1616 to provide ☞

'a butt of Sherry Sack' (about 700 bottles) to the first Poet Laureate, Ben Jonson.

England is the largest and most populous country of the United Kingdom – more than 83 per cent of the total UK population live there.

Gibraltar

✳Gibraltar
✳30,000
✳English, Spanish

Gibraltar lies on the south coast of Spain at the western entrance to the Mediterranean Sea.

Did you know?

The rock monolith of Gibraltar was formed by a massive upheaval of the earth about 200 million years ago; the top ridge was once far below the sea and is made from millions of compressed seashells. Admiral Nelson fought the Battle of Trafalgar against the French and Spanish near the western end of the Strait of Gibraltar – he won but was fatally wounded and his body was taken to Rosia Bay on Gibraltar before being sent back to England for burial (as the journey took so long in those days his body was sent back in a barrel of brandy to preserve it).

Guernsey

✳St Peter Port
✳64,000
✳English

Guernsey is the second largest of the Channel Islands and is situated 80 miles south of the English mainland.

Did you know?

The French writer Victor Hugo wrote *Les Misérables* whilst living in Hauteville House on Guernsey after his exile from France in 1851. He lived there until 1870.

Isle of Man

✳Douglas
✳74,000
✳English

The Isle of Man lies in the Irish Sea less than 60 miles west of the county of Lancashire in England.

Did you know?

It was originally part of the Norwegian kingdom of the Hebrides until the thirteenth century when it was ceded to Scotland and finally became part of the British Isles in 1765. The Manx language which was spoken by the first inhabitants is closely linked to Irish and Scots Gaelic. It remained the everyday language until the first half of the nineteenth century.

Jersey

✳St Helier
✳89,000
✳English, French

Jersey is part of the Channel Islands and is situated about 14 miles from the coast of France and about 100 miles south of the United Kingdom.

Did you know?

Gerald Durrell, writer and naturalist, founded the internationally known Jersey Zoo (now renamed as Durrell Wildlife) in 1958. The popularity of his book *My Family and Other Animals* enabled him to fund the project.

Malta

✳Valletta
✳394,000
✳Maltese, English

Malta is an archipelago in the central Mediterranean Sea south of Sicily.

Did you know?

Malta's megalithic temples are said to be the oldest in the world – older than England's Stonehenge and the pyramids of Egypt – dating back to 2,500 years BC.

The people of Malta were awarded the George Cross (one of the United Kingdom's highest awards for bravery) in 1942 – it was the first time the award had ever been made to a whole country, and recognised the island's bravery under attack during the Second World War.

Northern Ireland
✳Belfast
✳1,700,000
✳English, Irish Gaelic, Ulster Scots
Northern Ireland is situated on the island of Ireland and is made up of six north-eastern counties.
Did you know?
The Giant's Causeway on the north-east coast is an area of over 40,000 rock columns which were formed from a volcanic eruption about 60 million years ago. In 1900 Belfast had the biggest shipyard in the world; the doomed ocean liner *Titanic* was built there by Harland & Wolff at a reported cost of £7.5 million.

Scotland
✳Edinburgh
✳5,120,000
✳English, Scots, Gaelic
Scotland forms the northern third of Great Britain and shares a land border to the south with England.
Did you know?
Scotland includes 787 islands as well as the mainland and most of these belong to island groups such as the Hebrides, the Orkneys and the Shetlands; only 62 are bigger than three square miles. Scotland has its own legal system and has had its own parliament since 1999. In 2004, Edwin Morgan was appointed Scotland's first Makar, or Poet Laureate.
There is now a website dedicated to forecasting the places in Scotland worst affected by midges.

The system has been developed by a team of scientists in Edinburgh – and is known as www.midgeforecast.co.uk!

Wales
✳Cardiff
✳2,900,000
✳English, Welsh
Wales is located in the south-west of Great Britain and bordered by the English counties of Cheshire, Shropshire, Herefordshire and Gloucestershire to the east.
Did you know?
Wales has not been politically independent since 1282 when it was conquered by Edward I of England but since 1999 has had its own independent assembly. The post of National Poet of Wales was established in May 2005. Professor Gwyn Thomas took over the post from Gwyneth Lewis in July 2006. Sir George Everest, the traveller and explorer was born in Breconshire in 1790. The Himalayan peak which bears his name is the highest in the world.

Europe
Fact Finder

Papua New Guinea

Australia

Oceania

Nauru

Kiribati

Solomon
Islands

Tuvalu

Vanuatu

Fiji

Samoa

Tonga

Niue

Cook
Islands

New Zealand

Joker as Told

Not a latch or lock could hold
a little horse we had,
not a gate or paddock.

He liked to get in the house.
Walk in, and you were liable
to find him in the kitchen
dribbling over the table
with a heap behind him

or you'd catch a hoof
right where it hurt bad
when you went in your bedroom.

He grew up with us kids,
played with us till he got rough.
Round then, they cut him,

but you couldn't ride him:
he'd bite your bum getting on,
kick your foot from the stirrup

and he could kick the spurs off
your boots. Almost hopped on with you,
and if he couldn't buck you
he'd lie down plop! and roll
in his temper, and he'd squeal.

He was from the Joker breed,
we called him Joker;
no joke much when he bit you
or ate the Monday washing.

They reckon he wanted to be
human, coming in the house.
I don't think so. I think he
wanted something people had.
He didn't do it from love of us.

He couldn't grow up to be a
full horse, and he wouldn't be a slave one.
I think he was looking for his childhood,
his foalhood and ours, when we played.

He was looking for the Kingdom of God.

Les Murray

Captain H. W. Leaf

Now there was a man, big in every way,
    a big heart, big in body, a great fighter.
        He was the stuff that legends are made of.
He was talked about whenever and wherever
    his former comrades got together.
        He didn't die in the normal way.
No bullet can kill a legend. He goes on
    living in men's hearts, inspiring, leading,
        setting an example of courage that never
surrenders. We knew the legend, how he had
    taken to the hills where he was training
        a loyal band of followers for the attack
that would drive the enemy from the island,
    and we wanted to believe it. We knew
        the official account of his death, how
he had led his company, unwittingly,
    beyond the start-line of an attack,
        and was killed crossing a bridge,
but the real part of him, his legend,
    lives on, whether his name is known or not.
        He lives in the hills rallying the dead.

Alistair Te Ariki Campbell

Oceania

Kadavu

Kadavu:
sandbay
the east wind
cools:
dropped mango
on rockplates.

The sea runs
its smooth reaches
at the bay:
menfish softly
dive in
its tissue.

Christmas is gone,
New Year is coming:
and I walk it
unworried.

Christmas is gone,
New Year is coming:
I can hear
falling fruit.

Daylight dips
away, sun-shrinking:
songs shift in
the filling
dark.
*Some unworded
heartscalm fills
this place.*

Daylight dips
away, light-leaving:
songs shift in
the long
dark.
*Some unworded
heartscalm fills
this place.*

Anonymous

I Funnel Up...

I funnel up,
earth-leaving:
I snap the palm flags
on the way.
I peer at the sky-forever.
I see two red clouds.
If they were nearer
That would be my song-colour.

Anonymous

Arere, Eiroworowin & Eomakan

By a breathless cay
held hot in heaven's arms
the man Arere lived
with his wife Eiroworowin
and their 10 puppy-happy children.

One day, like every day,
a hot, wet day, Arere padded off
to fish the breathless cay
and Eiroworowin sat
skinning in the door.

Arere padded home,
one lapis fish goggling on his stick,
and went inside. 1 2 3 4 5 6 7 8 9.
'One of the children has gone.'
'Eomakan came,' said his wife.
The day still hot in heaven's arms.

Another day, like every day,
a hot, wet day, Arere padded off
to fish the breathless cay
and Eiroworowin sat
skinning in the door.   >

<

Arere padded home,
two lapis fish goggling on his stick,
and went inside. 1 2 3 4 5 6 7 8.
'Another child has gone.'
'Eomakan came,' said his wife.
The day more hot in heaven's arms.

Every day, like every day,
a hot, wet day, Arere padded off
to fish the breathless cay
and Eiroworowin sat
skinning in the door.

Arere padded home,
more lapis fish goggling on his stick,
and went inside. 7 6 5 4 3 2 1.
'Another child has gone,'
'Eomakan came,' said his wife.
Every day hotter in heaven's arms.

One day, like every day,
a hot, wet day, Arere padded off
and hid behind a prickled bush.
Rain nailed down on his grass hat.
He waited for Eomokan to come.

The shellsand shook. Shining with rain.
Eomakan stamped along the breathless cay.
'Eiroworowin! Where's Arere?'
'Fishing the lapis fish,' she said.
'Chuck me your child
or I'll come in and eat your everything!'

But Eiroworowin sat
skinning in the door.
Eomakan stamped inside
and felt the hot, wet air
with his creamy fingers.

Arere padded in behind
and chucked a raindropped net
around his childhot head.
Eiroworowin cut his windpipe with shells.
The day on fire in heaven's arms.

By the breathless cay
Eiroworowin sat
skinning in the door.
Arere laid the lapis fish
around the more nutritious meat
for stew. The rain came down.

Anonymous

The Magpies

When Tom and Elizabeth took the farm
  The bracken made their bed,
And *Quardle oodle ardle wardle doodle*
  The magpies said.

Tom's hand was strong to the plough
  Elizabeth's lips were red,
And *Quardle oodle ardle wardle doodle*
  The magpies said.

Year in year out they worked
  While the pines grew overhead,
And *Quardle oodle ardle wardle doodle*
  The magpies said.

But all the beautiful crops soon went
  To the mortgage-man instead,
And *Quardle oodle ardle wardle doodle*
  The magpies said.

Elizabeth is dead now (it's years ago)
  Old Tom went light in the head;
And *Quardle oodle ardle wardle doodle*
  The magpies said.

The farm's still there. Mortgage corporations
  Couldn't give it away.
And *Quardle oodle ardle wardle doodle*
  The magpies say.

Dennis Glover

Oceania

The Hurricane Love Songs 1

I now chance the night to write a song
that wanders in the personality of mist
korimoko slipping out of unwanted clothes
drops of water shaped like lit candles

If I was
If I was to tell you
If I was to tell you that I was born without
a bird pecking at my teeth, the kowhai
at the precious windows, a field of yellow
light and jocular roads ending at my eyes
would you believe me?

Then it is settled
I came to these shores barcly able to reach the belly
of my mother.
My feet already clad in soil with
a history of the koho and the smell of tyres,
a futureless beach at the end of the journey
a junction full of ships and floral dresses
as I am carried off the vessel
to stand on a platform rained on in the night.

I have since studied my hands
one side is white as the moon
a soft illusion curled at the lips
the other side is dark as your eyes

Never mind I keep telling myself
I have grown up here in a certain uncomfortable space
my shadow casts a question on the secret air
If I should drop everything I had found at the door

John Pule

Our island is holy

Our island is holy,

Being even as it came from Creator.

It is lovely, beyond

Any singing of it,

Watched by its hills

Grand and beautiful

Running gradually into the sea.

John Trevor Kason

Oceania

Prescription

Gather some sunshine

and warm rain

one cicada

and a pocket of air from your kitchen

a pot pourri of frangipani, sandalwood, mosooi

and gardenia

into a parcel

with a long letter

airmail

to me

from you

home in Samoa

Emma Kruse Vaai

This johnny...

This johnny
is Mr Strong from Strongtown.
He's got the government by the whatsits
He's got the prime minister by the whatsits
because he's the johnny
that runs the Big Men
he's the johnny that runs them round.
He opens all the Big Men's mouths
and they all talk Mr Strong talk
He candycakes all the Big Men's tongues
and they all talk Mr Sweet talk
He unshuts all the Big Men's eyes
And they all see Mr Strong's Progress Highway Go Now!

This johnny
is a friend of mine
Mm he wears all the gear
and all the flash jangles that go with the gear
But he's got me by the whatsits too
He's got me running all over the show too
oh looking for work work work
and working working working working
till I'm just a bunch of bones Ah

This johnny
is Mr Dollar.

Celo Kalagoe

Oceania

When we tell

I know English was brought
by White people to our country.
But when WE speak it,
when we slur that language like sinews
of vine floss extracting our teeth,
grind it with coral and ironwood in our mouths.
When WE tell of the gritty taste,
we've got to have a Tongan way
of doing it.

Loa Niumeitolu

I Wish ...

I wish I was
a dragonfly
hallelujah
in sungleam

Anonymous

and then night fell

in the beginning
it was hard:

men worked all day
all day was all

always day
always work

the sun spun
unmoved afloat

hung between
heaven and earth

nothing changed
nothing moved

always day
always work

and all the crickets
lived in heaven

whirring in a silent sheen
of lemon light

and men worked
and nothing changed

all day was all
all day was all   >

<

and one day
in the one day

in the silent sheen
of heaven

a lemon man
with legs of light

picked a cricket
out of a yellow breeze

and put it carefully
in his cricket-creel

and the gold toffee
floor of heaven

creaked and cracked
cracked and crackled

with the weight
of that one more cricket

the lemon man
belonged in heaven

and while the floor
creaked and cracked

he took hold of
a shining breeze

and saved himself
a hole cracked in the floor

his legs of light
dangled in the all day

and scrambled back
to heaven

and the cricket-creel
tumbled through the sky

down and down and down
past the sun

hung between
heaven and earth

and the working men
looked up

their diggers still
in amazed arms

and watched
the cricket-creel

tumble through the sky
and bang!

Oceania

they watched amazed
nothing moved nothing changed

and then
the crickets

one by one
whirring out

like flakes of light
from heaven

flickered at the
trees and grass

and sat
and sang

and something moved
something changed

the all day dimmed
the blue sky turned

grinding like
a grinding-stone

the sun rolled down
and then night fell

and the men
stopped working

and watched night fall
and hurried home

their diggers cold
in amazed arms

and sang themselves
and slept

and every day
has every night

when crickets sing
then night falls

and men stop work
and sleep.

Anonymous

Oceania

✳Capital
✳Population
✳Languages

Australia
✳Canberra
✳19,750,000
✳English

Australia is bounded by the Southern, Indian and Pacific Oceans with Indonesia, East Timor, Papua New Guinea, Solomon Islands, Vanuatu and New Zealand included in its list of neighbours.

Did you know?

The Great Barrier Reef is one of the wonders of the natural world; it is made up of over 2,800 coral reefs and is the largest reef system in the world at over 2,000 kilometres long. The best-known Australian song 'Waltzing Matilda', was written by a poet called 'Banjo' Paterson in 1895 and published in 1903.

Cook Islands
✳Avarua (on Rarotonga)
✳20,000
✳English, Maori

The Cook Islands archipelago lies in the South Pacific.

Did you know?

The British navigator Captain Cook named the islands the Hervey Islands in the 1770s but they were renamed the Cook Islands in his

honour about a century later by the Russians when they published a naval chart.

The most famous of the limestone caves on the island of Atiu is Antakitaki which is the home of the kopeka, a rare bird, similar to a swift, which lives only on this island.

Fiji
✳Suva
✳839,000
✳English, Fijian, Hindustani

Fiji is an island nation in the South Pacific Ocean, east of Vanuatu and west of Tonga.

Did you know?

Three hundred islands make up the Republic of Fiji but only about one third of them are inhabited.

The Dutch explorer Abel Tasman was the first European to discover the islands in 1643.

Kiribati
✳Tarawa
✳88,000
✳I-Kiribati, English

Kiribati is an island nation located in the central Pacific Ocean.

Did you know?

The International Date Line, an imaginary line which sits on the 180 degree longitude in the middle of the Pacific Ocean and marks the change from one day to the next, bends round to the east of these islands so that all of its islands can be in the

same time zone. The country has 33 low-lying coral islands scattered over an area roughly the size of the United States. Twenty-one of them are inhabited.

Nauru
✳Nauru
✳13,000
✳Nauruan, English

Nauru, formerly known as Pleasant Island, is an island republic in the Pacific Ocean.

Did you know?

It is one of the world's smallest independent countries both in terms of population and land area and is the only nation in the world with no official capital. Nauru had such huge reserves of phosphate built up from thousands of years of sea bird droppings that when they first started to mine the mineral, which is used in fertilizers, animal feeds and household detergents, it was probably the richest republic per person in the world.

New Zealand
✳Wellington
✳3,875,000
✳English, Maori

New Zealand is a country in the south-western Pacific Ocean made up of two large islands, North and South Island and a number of smaller islands.

Did you know?

The number of sheep outnumbers its people by about 10 to 1 although it used to be much higher, reaching its recorded peak in 1982 at over 70 million. The famous All Blacks rugby team perform the Maori *Haka* at the beginning of matches to strike fear into the hearts of their opponents – the dance ends with an all important throat-cutting gesture.

Niue
✳Alofi
✳2,000
✳English, Niuean

Niue is located north-east of New Zealand in a triangle between Tonga, Samoa and the Cook Islands.

Did you know?

Its name (pronounced new-ay) means 'behold the coconut' and although Captain Cook named it 'Savage Island', it is known as one of the Pacific's friendliest islands.

Papua New Guinea
✳Port Moresby
✳5,700,000
✳English and Tok Pisin (Pidgin)

Papua New Guinea lies north of Australia and west of the Solomon Islands and shares a border with Indonesia.

Did you know?

Sixteenth-century Portuguese explorers named New Guinea, Ilhas dos Papuas

Oceania
Fact Finder

(Island of the Fuzzy-Hairs) from the Malay word *papuwah*. Later, Spanish navigator Ynigo Ortis de Retez named it New Guinea (likening it to West Africa's Guinea) and the names were combined at independence in 1975.

It is difficult to find sources of protein for food in many parts of Papua New Guinea because of the limited animal life, so you may be offered delicacies like skewered sago grubs (with or without the heads) or roasted flying fox for dinner.

Samoa
✳Apia
✳178,000
✳Samoan, English
Samoa is located about halfway between Hawaii and New Zealand in the South Pacific.

Did you know?
It is an archipelago of nine islands and its name, from 'Sa' (sacred) and 'Moa' (centre) means 'Sacred Centre of the Universe'. Samoans have maintained their tradition of tattooing – it is often considered a

mark of manhood and cultural indentity. The male tattoo normally covers the man's body from the waist to the knees and is so dense it often looks like a pair of trousers!

Solomon Islands
✳Honiara
✳477,000
✳English, Melanesian, Pidgin
The Solomon Islands are an archipelago in the south-west Pacific.

Did you know?
The Solomon Islands are one of the friendliest places in the Pacific, but… head-hunting, cannibalism and skull worship were common right up to the 1930s! The Solomons are home to the chicken-sized megapode (so-called because of its large feet) which lays its eggs in hot, volcanic sand, crocodiles, flying foxes and rats bigger than domestic cats.

Tonga
✳Nuku'alofa
✳110,000
✳Tongan, English
The kingdom of Tonga lies in the south-west Pacific and is made up

of some 170 islands.
Did you know?
The islands, also known as the Friendly Islands, were so-named by Captain Cook in the late eighteenth century. He never realised that the islanders' friendliness to him was part of a plot (which failed) to steal the riches they had seen on his ships.

Tuvalu
✳Funafuti
✳11,000
✳Tuvaluan, English
Tuvalu, formerly known as the Ellice Islands, is a group of islands lying south of the equator in the western Pacific Ocean.

Did you know?
It has the smallest number of inhabitants (excluding the Vatican City) amongst independent nations and its highest point is unnamed, but officially recorded at 5 metres!

Vanuatu
✳Port Villa
✳212,000
✳English, Bislama (English Creole), French
Vanuatu is an

archipelago of some 80 islands in the south-west Pacific, lying east of Queensland in Australia and south of the Solomon Islands.
Did you know?
The earliest known settlement is on the Malo Islands, where pottery around 3,000 years old was unearthed.

James Cook, the British navigator, charted the islands in 1774 and called them the New Hebrides after the Scottish islands. The name was changed to Vanuatu in 1980 when the islands gained independence.

Sources and Acknowledgements

Our thanks are due to those authors and publishers who have kindly given permission to include or reproduce works.

EVERY EFFORT HAS BEEN MADE to trace the copyright holder of poems published in this book. If any material has been included without the appropriate acknowledgement, the publishers will be grateful of any notification or additions that should be incorporated in the next edition of this volume.

Poems by Leonidas Malenis, 'Golden Green Leaf' © 2007; Neil McCrindle, 'The Rock' © 2007; Yachitha Sahitra Samaraweera, 'Killer Waves' © 2007; Nitin Shroff, 'Out' © 2007; Joan Tapley, 'Do you know who Whatsisname is?' © 2007; Donna Triggs, 'Balancing Act' © 2007; Nondakofa Tujeni, 'Animal Freedom' © 2007; Dale Marie Witt, 'Listen to the Beat of the Sea' © 2007 are published by permission of the authors.

Patricia J. Adams, 'Rum Jumbee' from *Windows to Yesteryear* (in association with Anguilla National Trust, 1998); Margaret Atwood, 'Snake Woman' from *Interlunar* (OUP, 1984) reprinted by permission of Curtis Brown Ltd; James Berry, 'A Story about Afiya' from *When I Dance* (Puffin, 1990) reprinted by permission of Peters, Fraser & Dunlop Group Ltd; Alistair Te Ariki Campbell, 'Captain H.W. Leaf' from *Whetu Moana, Contemporary Polynesian Poetry in English* eds Albert Wendt, Robert Sullivan & Reina Whaitiri (Auckland University Press, 2003) reprinted by permission of the author; Peggy Carr, 'Flight of the Firstborn' from *Honey and Lime* (Virtualbookworm, 2006) reprinted by permission of the author; Yvette Christianse, from 'The Name of the Island' from *Castaway* (Duke University Press, 1999); John Cremona, 'Children Playing' from *New Voices of the Commonwealth* ed. Howard Sergeant (Evans, 1968); Malcolm de Chazal, 'it was/so hot...' from *The Song Atlas* ed. John Gallas (Carcanet, 2002) reprinted by permission of Carcanet Press Ltd; Noemia de Sousa, 'If you want to know me' from *Birthright: A Selection of Poems from Southern Africa* ed. Musaemura Bonas Zimunya (Longman International Education, 1990); U.A. Fanthorpe, 'Earthed' from *Collected Poems 1978-2003* (Peterloo Poets, 2005) reprinted by permission of Peterloo Poets; W. H. Gill, 'The Harvest of the Sea' from *Folklore of the Isle of Man* by Margaret Killip (Batsford, 1986) reprinted by permission of Anova Books Ltd; Denis Glover, 'The Magpies' from *Selected Poems* (Victoria University Press, 1995) reprinted by permission of the Denis Glover Estate © Pia Glover; Seamus Heaney, 'Personal Helicon' from *Death of a Naturalist* (Faber & Faber, 2006) reprinted by permission of Faber & Faber Ltd; dom Sylvester Houédard, 'Cosmic Text' reprinted by permission of the Trustees of Prinknash Abbey; Rashida Islam, 'Mon-doria' from *Daughters of a Riverine Land* ed. Debjani Chatterjee & Ashoka Sen (Sahitya Press, 2003) reprinted by permission of the author; Ingrid Jonker, 'The child who was shot dead by soldiers at Nyanga' from *World Poetry, An Anthology of Verse from Antiquity to Our Time* eds K. Washburn & John S. Major (W. W. Norton & Co., 1998); Celo Kalagoe, 'This johnny' from *The Song Atlas* ed. John Gallas (Carcanet, 2002) reprinted by permission of Carcanet Press Ltd; John Trevor Kason, 'our island is holy' from *Youth Writers 1971* ed. Marcia Kirstein (AH & AW Reed, 1971) reprinted by permission of Reed Publishing New Zealand; Knolly La Fortune, 'Carnival Rhapsody' from *Voice Print, Poetry from the Caribbean* eds Stewart Brown & Mervyn Morris (Longman Caribbean Writers Series, 1989); Kojo Laing, 'Senior Lady Sells Garden Eggs' from *Uncommon Wealth, An Anthology of Poetry in English* ed. Neil Bensner (OUP Canada, 1977); Madeleine Lee, 'First anniversary' from *A Single Headlamp: Poems by Madeleine Lee* (Firstfruits Publications, 2003); E.A. Markham, 'The Boy of the House' from *Ranters, Ravers and Rhymers* ed. Farrukh Dhondy (Collins, 1990) reprinted by permission of David Higham Associates; Claude-Joseph M'bafou-Zetebeg, 'The Free Bird' from *Talking Drums, Anthologie Africaine; A Selection of Poems from Africa south of the Sahara* trans. Veronique Tadjo (A & C Black, 2001) reprinted by permission of A & C Black Ltd; Felix Mnthali, 'Sunrise above Naisi' from *Birthright: a Selection of Poems from Southern Africa* ed. Musaemura Bonas Zimunya (Longman International Education, 1990) reprinted by permission of the author; Edwin Morgan, 'Canedolia' from *Collected Poems* (Carcanet, 1990) reprinted by permission of Carcanet Press Ltd; Micere Githae Mugo, 'Wife of the Husband' from *The Heinemann Book of African Women's Poetry* (Heinemann International Literature, 1995); Les Murray, 'Joker as Told' from *The daylight moon* (Carcanet, 1988) reprinted by permission of Carcanet Press Ltd; Grace Nichols, 'Wha Me Mudder Do' from *The Fat Black Woman's Poems* (Virago, 2006) reprinted by permission of Curtis Brown Ltd; Loa Niumeitolu, 'When We Tell' from *Whetu Moana, Contemporary Polynesian Poetry in English* eds Albert Wendt, Robert Sullivan & Reina Whaitiri (Auckland University Press, 2003) reprinted by permission of the author; Edward C. Okwu, 'Confession' from *New Voices of the Commonwealth* ed. Howard Sergeant (Evans, 1968); John Pule, 'The Hurricane Love Songs' from *Whetu Moana, Contemporary Polynesian Poetry in English* eds Albert Wendt, Robert Sullivan & Reina Whaitiri (Auckland University Press, 2003) reprinted by permission of the author; Taufiq Rafat, 'I am glad to be up and about' from *First Voices* (OUP Lahore, 1965); Savithri Rajeevan, 'A Pair of Glasses' from *The Oxford Anthology of Modern Indian Poetry* (OUP Delhi, 1996); Mohamad Haji Salleh, 'Home' from *New Voices of the Commonwealth* ed. Howard Sergeant (Evans, 1968); Barolong Seboni, 'All the Same' from Poetry Africa Festival, 2004 (www.nu.ac.za/cca); Alan Smith, 'Emily Hurricane' from *Under the Moon and Over the Sky: A Collection of Caribbean poems* eds John Agard and Grace Nichols (Walker Books, 2002) reprinted by permission of the author; Tejani, 'Night Illusion' from *New Voices of the Commonwealth* ed. Howard Sergeant (Evans, 1968); R.S. Thomas, 'Cynddylan on a Tractor' from *An Acre of Land, Collected Poems 1945-1990* (Phoenix, 1993) reprinted by permission of Orion Books Ltd; Turner Telcine, 'Morning Break' from *Can I buy a slice of sky? Poems from Black, Asian and American Indian Cultures* ed. Grace Nichols (Knight Books, 1993); Emma Kruse Vaai, 'Prescription' from *Whetu Moana, Contemporary Polynesian Poetry in English* eds Albert Wendt, Robert Sullivan & Reina Whaitiri (Auckland University Press, 2003) reprinted by permission of the author; Derek Walcott, 'A Sea-Chantey' from *Collected Poems 1948-1984* (Faber & Faber, 1992) reprinted by permission of Faber & Faber Ltd.

The following poems (Anon.): 'A Twist of Hair'; 'and then night fell'; 'Arere, Eiroworowin & Eomokan'; 'Careful!'; 'doodle durdle'; 'I Funnel Up...'; 'I wish...'; 'In the Woods'; 'Kadavu'; 'makeme'; 'My dugout flibbles'; 'Peace, Rain, Plenty'; 'Sleep-song'; 'The candy-throated Carib flaps...'; 'The Muiveyo Cow'; 'The Ten-Day Visitor'; 'When a fish...'; 'You' are from *The Song Atlas* ed. John Gallas (Carcanet, 2002) and are reprinted by permission of Carcanet Press Ltd. 'Children, Children' from *Skip Across the Ocean: Nursery Rhymes from around the World* ed. Floella Benjamin (Frances Lincoln, 1995).